# SAINTS

# SAINTS

Priya Hemenway

EVERGREEN

© 2007 TASCHEN GmbH
Hohenzollernring 53, D-50672 Köln
**www.taschen.com**

© 2006 by Book Laboratory Inc.

Lay out: Amy Ray

Production English edition:
Textcase, Hilversum, Netherlands
Typesetting cover for Textcase:
Elixyz Desk Top Publishing, Groningen, Netherlands

Printed in Singapore

ISBN-13: 978-3-8228-1597-7
ISBN-10: 3-8228-1597-7

# Contents

# Who are the Saints?

Two thousand years ago a most remarkable event took place. In the small town of Nazareth a man named Jesus began to speak to the people of Israel of love and compassion. He spoke to them of forgiveness, humility, and trust, and the words he spoke were delivered in a voice that was impossible to forget.

This man Jesus was eventually nailed upon a wooden cross to die, for the truths he spoke were unsettling. Large crowds gathered to listen to him, and many proclaimed him to be some sort of savior, without perhaps understanding that the devotion that was growing in their hearts would crucify the man they loved above all others. Perceiving the multitudes that assembled to hear this man speak, the authorities of the time—Jewish priests and Roman soldiers—grew apprehensive for their own ability to control and rule. Fearful they might be unseated they did what those in power so often do, they had Jesus killed.

Innocent of any crime, he was taken to the top of a hill and nailed upon a cross for all to see—like a common criminal. Above his head was placed a mocking sign that called him King of the Jews, and it was presumed that those who had gathered to hear him speak would take this epithet as an indication that following in his footsteps was not an option. It was intended to silence a voice the authorities did not want to hear. But the voice of Jesus was not silenced by this dastardly act. In fact, the crucifixion of this humble man took on a new and unexpected meaning. It became a symbol, not only of the purity of his innocence, but also of the transformation his words made possible.

At the end of the day the dead body of Jesus was taken down from the cross and buried, but the spirit of his words and the flame in his heart lived on. The truths of which he had spoken and the love with which he cared for humanity had already begun to play upon the spirit of those who had reached out to follow him. There were many whose lives were forever transformed.

As has always been the way of those who preach of love and inner wisdom, Jesus had a particularly strong influence on a close group of disciples. There were twelve men whom he drew close to himself and to whom he passed a sort of torch. These twelve men later became known as his apostles and they went out into their communities and traveled to other lands after his death, speaking of what had happened in Jerusalem. They announced to the world that this man Jesus, whom they also called Christ, had spoken words of such wisdom that, when taken to heart, brought a person closer in spirit to the mercy and compassion of God.

The God of whom they spoke became, in their words, a father to mankind. The God of Jesus, they said, is a loving God whose mercy is greater than it is possible to comprehend. The God of Jesus, they said, will transform the lives of all those who, with love in their hearts, draw near to Him.

With these ideas, Jesus and the disciples who followed him effected one of the most far-reaching changes to spiritual thought the world has ever known. Having tasted in his presence the joy and the peace of which he preached, the disciples of Jesus had themselves been transformed. They, too, began to live in the spirit of their teacher, and they experienced for themselves the truths of which he spoke.

It was their own experience that they referred to when they preached of the transforming power of love. It was their own experience that gave them the strength to suffer deaths that were similar to that of their teacher—for in every land there were men in powerful positions who were not willing to tolerate the spreading of such a message.

The men and women who have followed in the footsteps of Jesus are known to us as the Christian saints. Having taken his message to heart they have discovered for themselves its truth. They have been transformed through love and in turn, with grateful hearts have conveyed the simple message to others. With the joy and enthusiasm that comes to those who are transformed by the teachings of Jesus, his message has been carried around the world.

Like a fire it spreads, and like a fire it burns. The message of Jesus is simple, but it is one of the most powerful known to mankind: It is a message of love.

In the two thousand years that have passed since the days in which Jesus actually spoke, much has been done to preserve the words that were heard by those who were there. Teachings have developed and a Church created to empower the simple message and keep it alive. Naturally, because of the enormous complexity of the human psyche much has been done to pollute and destroy both the message of Jesus and his Church. Two thousand years have seen the emergence of a complex world, and the saints of Christ's message of love have found themselves faced with an ever-changing struggle against those in power who would try to have the message destroyed.

The message of Jesus is a message of love, and love carries with it certain properties. Love unseats malice and fear. Love blows like fresh air and has a course of its own. Love protects what is weak in the face of destruction and is in itself a strength more powerful than any might.

The saints of Christ's message have proved this. In different ways, at different times, over hundreds and hundreds of years, they have unfolded a history of extraordinary love and devotion. From martyrs to hermits, from teachers to legendary heroes, and from visionaries to samaritans, the saints of Christianity have created a tapestry of such rich and colorful tales that there seems no limit to the expressions that love might take. Real men and women, the saints live on in our hearts. They are kept alive because of a mysterious power they have. When we invoke their help we feel their grace, when we contemplate their deeds we are spiritually nourished, and when we dwell upon the eternal truth of their message, we continue always to be nurtured by the strength of their devotion.

*Saints* portrays only a handful of the many men and women who are known to us as saints, and they are given only a fraction of the space they really deserve. In order to give a greater understanding of their qualities, these forty-five saints that are mentioned are grouped under headings that briefly describe some of their main attributes. These headings also serve to give a broad view of some of Christianity's history.

The stories of the saints and the art that is used to illustrate them come from a variety of sources. Some saints lived long before accurate historical accounts were kept and some are so legendary there is no way to verify their existence. Others are of course known for their writings, and the lives of a few have been recorded by those who knew them well. For the most part the stories that are told and the art that is used here are recognized and are well established. There may be instances where this is not the case, and as with life, there are numerous sides to every story and discrepancies in every tale. Let this be the case with the stories of the saints in this little book. One thing is universally true of them all: Their love has made our world richer.

*If the only prayer*
*you say in your entire life*
*is "Thank You,"*
*that would suffice.*
*– Meister Eckhart (1260-1327)*

# Angels

The English word "angel" comes from the Greek angelos, which means "messenger." Like all religions Christianity is concerned with the relationship that human beings have with the supernatural—the realm in which we meet God, the realm in which transformation happens.

This relationship with the supernatural is thought to involve divine messengers sent to us to instruct, inform, or command. The angels are pure spirit, meaning that they have no material body. Their messages are very clear but are heard only by those who have ears with which to hear.

The names of the Archangels end with the suffix "el" which means "in God." The most popular Archangels are Michael, Raphael, Gabriel and Uriel. Michael (he who is like God), is the angel of mercy, repentance, and righteousness. Raphael (healing power of God) is the angel of prayer and love. Gabriel (strength of God) is the archangel of revelation. Uriel (light of God) is the archangel of transformation and enlightenment.

# Saint Michael the Archangel

A story is told of a great battle in Heaven in which the wicked angels, under the demon Lucifer, revolted against God. Michael, leading the faithful angels, defeated the evil hosts and drove them out. Because of this victory, the ancient Jews regarded the angel Michael as the special protector of Israel. In Christian usage he became the protector of the Church.

Saint Michael has four duties:
- To continue to wage battle against all that is evil in the world.
- To save the souls of the faithful especially at the hour of death.
- To protect the people of God.
- To lead the souls of those recently departed from this life and present them for judgment.

He is often portrayed holding a scale in his hand, with which he weighs and determines the innocence of each soul.

# Saint Gabriel the Archangel

The Bible records several appearances by the archangel Gabriel. He was twice sent to the prophet Daniel. On the second occasion Daniel was at prayer, and Gabriel prophesied the date of the first coming of the Messiah. Because of this there was great expectation among the Jews at the time when Jesus was about to be born, and this was heightened by the appearances of Gabriel to Zacharias the priest and husband of Elizabeth, mother of John the Baptist, and then to Mary, who was betrothed to Joseph and gave birth to Jesus.

When Jesus was born in Bethlehem, his birth was the signal for a glorious witness of divine approval that was seen by shepherds in a nearby field. As an angel appeared to them they were filled with fear. Suddenly there was with the angel "a multitude of the heavenly host praising God and saying, 'Glory to God in the highest, and on earth peace and good will toward men.'"

# Biblical Figures

Participating in the life of Jesus were the earliest of the people we know of as of saints. Angels and prophets announced his coming; Mary gave birth to him; and close relations during his lifetime devoted their hearts to his teaching. The people and the events of Jesus' life have been sanctified. Those who were close were blessed, for they acknowledged his divinity and, during his life, partook of his wisdom and love.

A long line of prophets had spoken to the Hebrew people during the hundreds of years that proceeded his birth. Isaiah, Jeremiah, Ezekiel, and Daniel—great prophets from the past—had announced him. John the Baptist, a prophet in Jesus' own lifetime, spoke fervently to great crowds preparing the way for him and proclaiming for all who could hear that "the Kingdom of Heaven is at hand." The prophets all knew in their hearts that a great revolution would be initiated with the arrival of Christ.

Mary, the Blessed Virgin, and the carpenter Joseph brought Jesus into this world. Elizabeth and Joachim were the parents of John the Baptist who baptized him. Together these saints speak to us of parental love, of devotion and trust. They represent perfection and the most sublime aspect of faith—a surrendered heart. With enormous humility, they cared for the innocent child who was to become the new Messiah.

Mary Magdalene, the friend and follower of Jesus, is a herald of the transformation that is possible through the love and guidance of Jesus, the master. As the first person to whom the arisen Christ presented himself, Mary Magdalene was blessed as a disciple and as a saint. As the one who, legend says, symbolically anointed the feet of her master, she performed an ancient rite in which grace descended upon her and kindled the flame of devotion.

# Saint Mary, Mother of Jesus

Perhaps the most beloved of all saints, Mary, or Miriam, represents the love and devotion of those who seek comfort and salvation through the Church.

As a young woman she lived in Nazareth and was betrothed to a man named Joseph. She was startled one day by the mysterious vision of the angel Gabriel who appeared to her saying, "Hail! The Lord is with you."

"Do not be afraid, Mary, for you have found favor with God. Behold, you will conceive in your womb and bear a son, and you shall name him Jesus. He will be great and will be called Son of the Most High, and the Lord God will give him the throne of David his father, and he will rule over the house of Jacob forever, and of his kingdom there will be no end."

Mary, who was still a virgin, said to the angel, "How can this be, since I have no relations with a man?" The angel replied that the Holy Spirit, in a wonderful and unfathomable mystery, would create within her womb a child and that this child would be known as the Son of God.

# Saint Elizabeth

Gabriel told Mary that Elizabeth, her cousin who was thought to be barren, had also conceived a son, explaining that nothing is impossible for God.

After Gabriel had left her, Mary went to visit Elizabeth and found her in the sixth month of a miraculously conceived pregnancy. As Mary entered the room the child inside of Elizabeth leapt for joy and Elizabeth was filled with some mystical understanding. "Blessed are you among women," she said to Mary, "and blessed is the fruit of your womb! And why is this granted me, that the mother of my Lord should come to me?"

Elizabeth's pregnancy was surprising because she and her husband Zachariah were old and had tried unsuccessfully to have a child. When Elizabeth found herself pregnant, her husband said nothing. He was a priest and had been serving one day at the temple when Gabriel appeared to him and greeted him with the news that he and his wife were to become parents. Zachariah was awestruck and asked for a sign, whereupon Gabriel informed him that he would be unable to speak until the predicted events came to pass. Zachariah became mute and could explain nothing to his wife.

# Saint John the Baptist

The child that that was born to Zachariah and Elizabeth is known to us as John the Baptist. He was the last of the prophets. As a young man John lived as a hermit in the desert of Judea. When he was about thirty he began to preach on the banks of the Jordan River against the evils of the times. He called people to penance and baptism saying that the "Kingdom of Heaven is close at hand."

One day Jesus approached John. Recognizing him as the Savior he had been announcing, John baptized him, saying, "It is I who need baptism from you." Then he addressed Jesus as the "Lamb of God who takes away the sins of the world," and acknowledged him as the Messiah. John inspired many of his own followers to follow Jesus.

Fearful of John's great power, Herod Antipas had him arrested and imprisoned at a fortress on the Dead Sea. John had denounced Herod's adulterous and incestuous marriage with Herodias and was beheaded at the vengeful request of Salome, the daughter of Herodias, who asked for his head in exchange for a dance she performed for Herod.

# Saint Mary Magdalene

Mary Magdalene is called "the Penitent" because of a story in Luke's Gospel later connected to her. When Jesus went to supper at the home of a rich man, she entered and bowing down at his feet, washed them with her tears. With her long hair, she then wiped them dry and anointed them with oil.

Jesus said to her "Your faith has made you safe; go in peace." Mary devoted herself to serving Jesus and she stood at the foot of the cross when he was crucified. After Jesus' body had been placed in the tomb, Mary went to anoint it with spices. Not finding the body, she began to weep, and seeing someone whom she thought was the gardener, she asked him if he knew where the body of her beloved master had been taken. The stranger spoke in a voice she knew well, and she recognized Jesus, risen from the dead.

Legend says that many years later, Mary was put in a boat without sails or oars. Accompanying her were several other close friends of Jesus. They were sent drifting out to sea and landed on the shores of Southern France, where Mary Magdalene spent the rest of her life meditating in a cave. It is said that angels fed her.

# Apostles

The apostles are the twelve men whom Jesus brought close to himself and chose to instruct more carefully. He treated them like brothers and prepared them to be sent out into the world with his message. (The Greek word apostolos means to send forth.)

Except for Matthew, who was a tax collector, these men were uneducated, mostly fishermen, and during their time with Jesus they were often unable to grasp the meaning of his teachings. Yet, they followed him everywhere, with their hearts opened by his love and their minds made clear by their devotion.

Jesus addressed their skepticism with small miracles and words of wisdom; and as they grew in love they participated in many extraordinary events. They listened to Jesus' sermons, watched as he healed the sick and tried to understand when he spoke in parables to the curious. Together with a number of other followers the apostles witnessed miraculous signs of his Godly presence and were present during his Sermon on the Mount when he described the blessings that await those who follow him.

The twelve apostles of Jesus were:

Simon, called Peter, "the rock"

Andrew, brother of Peter

John, the son of Zebedee

James the Elder or "Greater," bother of John

Philip

Matthew, sometimes called Levi

Bartholomew

Thomas, also known as Didymus or "the twin"

James the Lesser, or "Younger," brother of Jude

Jude Thaddaeus, sometimes called Matthew Lebbaeus

Simon the Canaanite, sometimes called "Simon the Zealot"

Judas Iscariot

The last of these, Judas Iscariot, betrayed Jesus just before his death and hanged himself in guilt before Christ's resurrection. The remaining apostles selected Matthias to fill his place by casting lots.

In the early days of Christianity all of Jesus' disciples were called "saints" and are credited with spreading Christianity through the various early churches.

# Saint Peter

A young fisherman known as Simon was named Peter (the "rock") by Jesus when he proclaimed, "Upon this rock I will build my Church." Peter is often called the Prince of Apostles. At the Last Supper Jesus said Peter would deny him, and after his arrest the frightened Peter swore three times that he did not know Jesus. Distressed at what he had done, Peter was later forgiven.

A well-known story tells of Saint Peter walking on water. He was out fishing when a storm arose, and at its height Jesus appeared, standing on the sea, and summoned him. Peter climbed out of the boat and began to walk. After a few moments he realized what he was doing and as doubt arose in his heart he sank into the water. Jesus pulled him out.

Towards the end of his days Peter was thrown into prison by King Herod Agrippa. One night he went to sleep and dreamed that his cell was filled with light. An angel came, took him by the hand, and led him out. As doors opened miraculously they passed guards who simply did not see them. Peter was convinced he was sleeping, but once outside the prison gates he opened his eyes and realized that this had not been a dream, and that he had been rescued.

# Saint Andrew

Andrew was Peter's brother and also a fisherman. One day he left his nets and walked for miles in search of the prophet John the Baptist who was preaching at the River Jordon. He was baptized by this charismatic man and was standing in the crowd when Jesus approached and John the Baptist recognized him as the Messiah. After Jesus' baptism, Andrew ran after him wanting to meet and learn more of this man.

He later brought his brother Peter to meet Jesus. Together with Peter and their cousin John, Andrew accompanied Jesus and his mother to a wedding feast at Cana. There the young men saw the first of many miracles in which Jesus turned water into wine. After the feast Andrew and Peter returned home to their fishing nets, but Jesus came after them saying, "Come follow me and I will make you fishers of men." Having become a disciple, it was Andrew who, at the gathering of a large crowd of five thousand, found a young boy whose few fish enabled Jesus to miraculously feed them all.

He is said to have suffered crucifixion on a form of the cross called Crux decussata (X-shaped cross) and commonly known as "Saint Andrew's cross."

# Saint James the Elder

James was called James the Elder to distinguish him from James the son of Alphaeus. One day he and his brother John sat mending their fishing nets with their father. They watched as their friends Simon and Andrew brought in nets loaded with fish and then walked away from their catch at a word from Jesus. Approaching James and John, Jesus then bade them do what their friends had done, and impulsively, without argument or discussion, James and John left their boat and their father behind and followed Jesus.

Once when some innkeepers refused accommodations to Jews, the outraged brothers asked Jesus to call down fire from heaven to avenge the insult. Jesus refused saying, "The son of man is not come to destroy men's lives, but to save them." After this, he called the brothers the "Sons of Thunder."

One day James and John told Jesus they wished to sit at his side when he came to glory. When Jesus replied that they didn't know what they were asking they tried another question: Could they could share his drinking cup? Jesus assured them that they could, and in the days that led up to his death, this promise was fulfilled. At the Last Supper they drank from his cup.

# Saint John

John, the son of Zebedee, and the brother of Saint James the Elder, became known as the "beloved disciple" and was the only one of the twelve who did not forsake Jesus in the hour of his passion. He was one of Jesus' dearest companions and during the Last Supper he sat at his right and later was present at Jesus' trial. In his final hours Jesus called to him from the cross, asking him to take care of his mother, Mary. "Woman, here is your son," he said, and to John, "Here is your mother."

On the night of his crucifixion, the body of the dead Christ was taken down from the cross, embalmed, and placed in a cave-like tomb, the entrance to which was sealed by a large stone. Three days later the tomb was empty and as one of the first to realize what had happened, with unshakable faith John proclaimed that his Master had risen from the dead.

In his later life he founded churches in Asia Minor. Tradition relates that he was brought to Rome and cast into a cauldron of boiling oil from which he emerged unhurt. He survived all his fellow apostles and lived to a very old age.

# Saint Thomas

The story of "Doubting Thomas" is well known, and indeed his doubt was natural, for Christ had been nailed to a cross, pierced with a spear, and buried in a tomb for three days. How could he be alive? When told of the appearance of the risen Christ, Thomas declared, "I will never believe it unless I see the holes the nails have made in his hands and put my fingers on the marks and my hand into his side." When Jesus appeared to him he cried "My Lord and my God!" asserting his belief in the divinity of Jesus.

The story of Thomas' doubt is really a story of his passionate trust in his Master. On an earlier occasion when Jesus had been forced out of Jerusalem because of his teachings, he received a message that his good friend Lazarus was gravely ill and possibly dead. Jesus prepared to go visit his friend who lived on the outskirts of Jerusalem regardless of the risk to himself. As he began his journey the disciples argued against it, reasoning that Lazarus was probably already dead and that the trip would serve no real end and would only cause them problems. It was Thomas who insisted upon the journey saying, "Let us go, that we may die with him."

# Saint James the Younger and Saint Jude

James and Jude were brothers and seem to have been related either to Joseph or to Mary. One story relates that James so resembled Jesus that it was difficult for those who did not know to tell them apart. This may explain why the kiss of Judas was needed on the night of Jesus' final arrest in the Garden of Gethsemane. It would certainly have been necessary to make certain that Jesus, and not James, was taken into custody by the soldiers.

Jude was also known as Thaddeus or Matthew Lebbaeus. The Aramaic meaning of both Thaddeus and Lebbaeus is "beloved" or "dear to the heart." One of the last questions Jesus answered had been put to him by Jude. Just before Jesus began his prayers in the Garden of Gethsemane, prior to his arrest, Jude asked how he will reveal himself to them in the future.

Jesus answered, "If a man loves me and obeys my teachings, my father and I will love him and we will come to him and abide with him."

# Evangelists

The evangelists are the men who wrote the four Gospels—the books in the Bible that tell the life story and teachings of Jesus. The Gospels provide the material that was to become the foundation of Christianity.

The word "gospel" literally means "good news," and until the early twentieth century they were mainly interpreted as biographies of Jesus. In more recent times it has been speculated that stories about his life and teaching were passed on orally and there may have been many different versions. It was the four evangelists who assembled the anecdotes and gave them order.

The evangelists are traditionally identified as Matthew, Mark, Luke, and John. The Gospels of the first three give a similar view of what had happened. The Gospel of John is quite different and was clearly written later than the other three. It is possible that someone who was inspired by Saint John's memories wrote it.

# Saint Matthew

Legend says that after Jesus' resurrection, Matthew remained in Palestine while the other apostles dispersed, and that he was urged to set down from memory the life and teachings of the Messiah. However, scholarly opinion says that he was probably a second generation disciple unrelated to the disciple Matthew and that this Gospel was written around the year 85 or 90 in Syria.

The Gospel of Saint Matthew addresses a community of Jewish and non-Jewish Christians and it attempts to make disciples of people from any faith. Beginning with the miraculous conception of Jesus, Matthew wrote his Gospel as a history of salvation, dividing his story into two parts—the period of prophecy and the period of fulfillment. Jesus' life is described as fulfilling a promise to both the people of Israel and to the people of a greater kingdom.

Matthew says that all those who follow Jesus will become children of God and that they will live in His kingdom until the end of time. This great kingdom, he continues, is available to to the people of all nations.

# Saint Mark

The Gospel of Saint Mark is the shortest of the four Gospels and was almost certainly the first to be written. It is usually dated as being written sometime between the years 65 and 75. Although the use of narrative to record spiritual history was common to the Jews, there are no parallels to this precise literary form before this time. In all probability Mark was responsible for creating the genre we know as "gospel."

Mark was a disciple of the second generation and legend connects him to both Peter and Paul with whom he appears to have gone on missionary trips. Most of what Mark writes he attributes to his teachers, recounting with great fervor the details of what they had witnessed. There were however, parts of the story that were difficult for him to resolve.

Very possibly written in Rome, Mark was addressing a community of people that were being made to suffer for their faith. They were having difficulty grasping the meaning of Jesus' resurrection. Mark explained to them that to follow in the footsteps of Jesus involves suffering persecution, but, he said, the implication of the resurrection is that they would be rewarded in heaven.

# Saint Luke

It is believed that Luke was born a Greek and a Gentile and that he was a medical man and an artist. A picture of the Virgin Mary was reportedly found in Jerusalem some years after his death that is believed to have been painted by Saint Luke.

Although Luke had not been an eyewitness to the events of Christ's life, some legends say he was a companion to Saint Paul on some of his early missions and later became a disciple. Luke would have listened carefully to all that he heard and then added his own twist to the story when he later wrote it down.

Not only did Luke give a full account of the life of Jesus, he went on afterwards to write the Acts of the Apostles. In this book, which now follows the four Gospels in the Bible, Luke attempted to tell a history of this new and growing faith that had started with a few people in Jerusalem. He pieced together all the information he could from stories the apostles told him.

The Gospel of Luke shows a clear intention to convert the Gentiles. It is only in this Gospel that we hear the parable of the Good Samaritan.

# Saint John

John is traditionally credited with having written three Epistles and one Gospel, although many scholars believe that the final editing of the Gospel was done by others some time after his death. Saint John's reminiscences would have provided accurate information about the ministry of Jesus, and a following that grew up around him in the town of Ephesus might well have completed his work.

John lived into his old age at Ephesus where he passed his days in prayer and contemplation, pondering the mysterious and mystical events of Jesus' life. Physically consumed with the love for him, it is said John preached a simple message. To those who gathered to be near the gentle soul and to hear him speak, John said simply, "Little children, love one another." When it was suggested he might vary his message, John was surprised and explained that this was Christ's essential message and that "If you keep it, you do enough."

# Martyrs

During the three hundred years that followed Jesus' crucifixion, his followers were captured, tortured, and killed. The most obvious reason for this was that the early Christians would not conform to the state religion—a stance that was considered treasonous. Ugly rumors were circulated about them, and they were often accused of taking part in secret meetings and strange rites.

During the reign of the Roman Emperor Nero their persecution reached a frenzied pitch after he blamed them for starting a huge fire in Rome. He had thousands of men and women put to death for refusing to acknowledge respect to Roman gods. Upper-class Christians were beheaded; the rest were burned or eaten by wild beasts.

Considering the end they met, it is no surprise that the martyrs were later commemorated as saints. Their bones were enshrined and their graves became places of prayer. The brutal deaths they suffered were seen as sacrifices that associated their lives and deaths with the life and death of Christ.

# Saint Stephen

Stephen was the first Christian to be martyred for his beliefs. His name means "crown," which refers to his wearing of the martyr's crown.

In the years that immediately followed the crucifixion of Jesus the early Church grew so rapidly that the apostles needed help with their work. They ordained seven men to help them, and Stephen was one of them.

The enemies of this early Church were displeased with its fast development and when they heard Stephen preaching they laid a plot for him. Innocent of any crime, he was brought before a council of the high priests in Jerusalem where false witnesses accused him of blasphemy. Saint Stephen faced that great assembly of enemies without fear, defending the Christian faith and explaining that Jesus Christ was indeed the Messiah. Even the members of the council saw in his face the look of an angel.

Stephen was subsequently dragged outside the city of Jerusalem and stoned to death.

# Saint Dionysius d. 258

Born and raised in Italy, Dionysius was sent as a missionary to Gaul sometime around the year 250 by Pope Clement. He set up his base of missionary activity on an island in the Seine near the city of Lutetia Parisorium, which would later become Paris.

While there he was captured by the Gauls along with the other missionaries who had accompanied him. They were accused and arrested. After a long imprisonment and several aborted executions Dionysius, along with two of his companions, were beheaded and their bodies were thrown to the wild beasts. Miraculously Dionysius rose to his feet, stooped over and picked up his head. Then he walked—with angels singing by the wayside—to the Mount of Martyrs (Montmartre) where the three bodies were buried.

Dionysius is known as the first bishop of Paris and the patron saint of France.

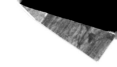

# Saint Thomas Becket (1118—1170)

At the age of twenty-four Thomas began his career in the Church. Due to his exceptional skills in diplomacy he became a close friend of the young King Henry II of England, and when the See of Canterbury fell empty King Henry announced to Thomas that he wished him to become the new archbishop. Thomas replied, "Should God permit me to be the archbishop of Canterbury, I would soon lose your majesty's favor. The affection with which you honor me would be changed into hatred." Sure enough, when Thomas opposed Henry over an ecclesiastical question he had to flee to France. The men were eventually reconciled by the pope and Thomas returned to England, but he immediately infuriated Henry again by excommunicating some bishops. Henry flew into a rage. Four knights seeking the favor of their king rode to Canterbury where they banged on the church doors.

"Away, you cowards! A church is not a castle," shouted Thomas, but they entered, beat Thomas to his knees, and killed him. When news of this was brought to King Henry, he shut himself up and fasted for forty days. Though far from faultless, Thomas Becket had the courage to lay down his life to defend the rights of the Church against an aggressive and powerful State.

# Virgin Martyrs

Stemming from an idea that took hold in the early days of the Christian Church, virgin martyrs have been honored with a very special reverence. Greek philosophers of the time encouraged the idea that women were in some way inferior to men. The early Church picked up on this and portrayed woman as the origin of sin.

The early Fathers said Eve represented the powers of seduction and sex, once considered a doorway to the divine, but now associated with the temptations that lead directly to hell.

Christian women, who could do nothing about the creative urge, suffered from a terrible repression. They were led to believe that to lose their virginity would render them incomplete and that association with them would be spiritually damaging to their partners. To support this theory the Church encouraged the veneration of virgin martyrs. Saint Ursula and Saint Catherine of Alexandria are only two of thousands that suffered a cruel death while defending their virginity.

# Saint Ursula

According to a legend that appeared in the tenth century, Ursula was the daughter of an early Christian king in Briton. He had arranged a marriage for her with a pagan prince—a marriage to which Ursula objected.

She talked her father into arranging a postponement of the ceremony, stipulating that if her suitor truly wished to marry her he must first support a pilgrimage to Rome in which she would be accompanied by ten thousand virgins. The prince complied, and Ursula set off with the virgins. After an extensive journey through Europe the group arrived in Cologne. There they were met by an invading horde of Huns.

Ursula urged the virgins to die at the sword rather than submit to sexual abuse by the Huns and offered herself as the first victim. All of the ten thousand virgins were massacred.

A church was eventually built in Cologne in honor of the virgins and the legend of Ursula grew. Several versions of the story are told.

# Saint Catherine of Alexandria

When Catherine was a young woman of eighteen years she attracted the attention of the Roman Emperor Maxentius, not for her remarkable beauty and outstanding intelligence but because she made a public point of protesting against the worship of idols. At one time she is said to have so ably defended her beliefs that she perplexed fifty of the Emperor's philosophers in a theological debate.

Maxentius proposed marriage to Catherine, but she refused. As a result she was beaten for two hours, imprisoned, and finally tied to a spiked 'Catherine' wheel from which we have developed the sputtering Catherine-wheel firework.

The wheel miraculously shattered and the two hundred soldiers who were watching promptly converted. In a rage Maxentius had them all beheaded along with Catherine. It is said that at her death milk flowed from her severed arteries. Since pre-Christian times, milk has been a symbol of fertility, nutrition, and healing and has been used most significantly in the image of the Virgin Mary suckling the Christ child.

# Founders and Educators

The hundreds of years that have seen the development of Jesus' message are full of founders, poets, educators, and writers. Their task was to keep the spirit of the message alive while they formed a context in which people could gather to share in celebration and to practice living the message of Christ. There are many saints whose work it was to give structure to the Church and to develop communities in which men and women could devote themselves to a life of prayer and contemplation. They spoke and wrote as ideas developed, and it is upon their work that much contemporary religious thought is based.

Peter and Paul were the earliest of the Church's founders. Traveling from place to place they began to formulate the ideas that, in the many years to come, would establish the new Christian religion as one of the world's great monotheistic traditions.

Rome at this time was the greatest power on Earth, a warring nation whose people revered a great pantheon of gods. Their military strength was unequaled and governance was cruel and unforgiving. The followers of Christ were spreading a message of love and compassion, and the message had great merit—but it was certainly not welcomed by the empire's elite who saw it as subversive. During the first four hundred years in which the early followers of Jesus were converting new believers to a new God, many signs that the Christian God had magic powers were imagined.

In 312, one of the two opposing rulers to the Roman Empire, Constantine, was preparing for battle. One story says that he had his doubts about the traditional gods and earnestly prayed that the true god would reveal who he was and would help him. Thereupon Constantine saw a cross of light in the sky and the inscription "*In hoc signo vinces*—In this sign you will win."

Accepting this as an answer to his prayer he had the sign of the cross inscribed on his soldiers' armor. He went to battle and was victorious. The Christians saw a change of heavenly allegiance, and the followers of Jesus ceased to be persecuted. Within seventy years Christianity was the official religion of the Roman Empire.

Around 400, however, the Empire began to weaken and northern tribes swept through Europe and plundered the city of Rome. The Roman Empire collapsed and was replaced by many small kingdoms. During the next one thousand years, through the period known of as the Middle Ages, the Church became the unifying force between these numerous small kingdoms, and oversaw the formation of what we now know as Europe.

During this time the popes of Rome grew in power, finally claiming complete authority over Christian Europe, dictating its political as well as its spiritual climate. The saints that emerged to give direction to this new Church walked a fine line between acceptance and excommunication. They were men and women with a great range of experience. Their ideas would change the way people viewed their existence.

As both popes and revolutionaries, the founders and educators of the Christian religion include Saints Peter and Paul, who set out with a mission of conversion, and Saint Jerome who, among many, helped with the evolution of our modern-day Bible. Saint Augustine and others like him were the eloquent authors of prosaic and poetic journals that articulated the passions that burned the Christian soul; meanwhile the logic of such saints as Thomas Aquinas formulated the tenents upon which the strengths of the Christian religion now rely.

# Saint Peter

Peter is often called Prince of the Apostles. Legends say that he was a founder, along with Saint Paul, of the Christian authority or Papal See of Rome. Jesus called him Cephas, which was the Aramaic word for "rock"—alluding to the rock upon which the new Church would be built, for Peter was the first person to profess the belief that Jesus was the Son of God.

An episode is recounted in the Gospel of Matthew that tells of Jesus asking his disciples who they thought he was. Peter answered, "You are the Messiah, the Son of the living God." To this Jesus said, "Simon son of Jonah, you are a blessed man! It was not human agency that revealed this to you, but my Father in heaven. So now I say to you: You are Peter, and on this rock I will build my community... I will give you the keys to the kingdom of Heaven: Whatever you bind on earth will be bound in heaven; and whatever you loose on earth shall be loosed in heaven."

After his death Jesus appeared before the disciples at Tiberias and gave his famous command to Peter, "Feed my lambs... Tend my sheep...."

# Saint Paul (3 - 65)

Originally called Saul, Paul converted to Christianity and became, with Peter, the legendary co-founder of the early Church of Rome. One of the most important figures in the early development of Christianity, Paul wrote extensively, and his thoughts had a profound influence on the early Church. He saw humans as naturally corrupt and believed that we are unable to save our own souls without the help and guidance of Christ.

Before his conversion, Saul was a Jew who hated and persecuted Christians. He had played a leading role in searching out members of the early Church and assisted in the stoning of Stephen, the first martyr. One day, while on his way to attack Christians in Damascus, Saul was thrown from his horse. As he lay on the ground he was blinded by a vision in which Jesus said to him that Saul's persecution of Christians was persecuting him. Three days later, Saul was miraculously cured of his blindness. Filled with the Holy Spirit he was soon baptized and changed his name to Paul in order to reflect a new beginning to his life.

# Saint Jerome (347 - 419)

Jerome was born to Christian parents who provided him with a model Roman education, arranging for lessons in grammar, Latin, and Greek and sending him to Rome to study under a famed grammarian. As he himself noted, "Almost from the very cradle I have spent my time among grammarians and rhetoricians and philosophers."

Inspired by the ethic of the Christian recluses Jerome became a monk and lived for three or four years among a small community of like-minded Christians in Italy. Provoked by a vision, he determined to prove his utter devotion by banishing himself to the wilderness. Try as he might, however, he could not give up his cherished library and passion for the written word.

So he left the desert and went to Antioch where the pope soon recognized his gifts as a biblical scholar and commissioned him to produce a new Latin translation of the Bible. By that time a confusing variety of scriptures in many different languages were in circulation throughout the young Church, many of them containing numerous inconsistencies. As Jerome later said "There were almost as many forms of the text as there were copies."

# Saint Augustine of Hippo (350 - 430)

Augustine spent his early years in loose living, and his change of heart and conversion have been an inspiration to many of those who struggle with habits they long to break.

Although he had been brought up as a Christian, Augustine was a deeply troubled young man. He had became convinced that Christianity was the best religion for him but he did not consider himself worthy, because he thought he could never live a pure life. One day he heard two men talking. They had read a life of Saint Anthony and were immediately converted. Augustine felt terribly ashamed of himself. "What are we doing?" he said to a friend "Unlearned people are taking heaven by force, while we, with all our knowledge, are so cowardly that we keep rolling around in the mud of our sins!"

He was baptized, became a priest, a bishop, and the famous writer of a collection called Confessions. "Our hearts were made for you, O Lord, and they are restless until they rest in you," he wote. Saint Augustine lived in poverty and supported the poor, preached often, and prayed with great fervor. He approached his death with the lament: "Too late have I loved you."

# Saint Thomas Aquinas (1225 - 1275)

Thomas' intention to become a mendicant friar shocked his parents so much that they tried to dissuade him by locking him in the family fortress for a year. Not to be deterred, he joined the Dominicans at the age of nineteen and went to Paris to study, becoming bald while still young and growing enormously fat. He is reputed to have had a crescent carved out of his dining table to accommodate his vast belly. Thomas had remarkable powers of concentration and at times would dictate to four secretaries simultaneously. His life was spent lecturing, studying, writing, and traveling until he died of exhaustion at the age of forty-nine.

Thomas' work was the summit of intellectual achievement in the Middle Ages. He studied Arabic, Judaic, and Christian texts, and then fused them into a comprehensive orderly exposition of theology. His scientific approach defined reason and faith as separate and complementary elements. Reason aids the understanding of belief he said, and faith starts where reason reaches its limits. The clarity and logic of his arguments is still recognized, and his major work Summa Theologica, although unfinished, became a standard theological text.

# Ascetics, Desert Fathers, Monks

When Christianity became established, believers no longer lived under the threat of persecution and martyrdom ceased to be an ultimate expression of faith. Consequently Christians endeavoring to attain spiritual perfection began to withdraw from the world to take up a life of solitude and asceticism.

Strictly speaking, asceticism is the suppression of the body for spiritual ends. The early Greeks, whose thought was very influential at that time, believed the human body to be inferior and corrupting, and the spirit alone to be pure. In order to attain the spiritual planes, it was believed that the body must be suppressed.

Despite the tremendous hardship that such a life implies, the early Christian ascetics practiced devotedly, and many of them began to discover great joys in their life of solitude. Trusting themselves to God, they learned lessons of humility and trust, and because there was little distraction they were faced with a deepening recognition of what was separating them from God. Praying continuously they learned to rejoice in the simple pleasures of their love.

Stories of hermits began to circulate, attracting followers who made pilgrimages to the deserts and wild places of Egypt, Syria, and Asia Minor to meet them and to become hermits themselves. Loosely organized communities grew up around charismatic elders, and the solitary tradition began to yield a communal way of life.

Some of these men and women were known as "anchorites" (from the Greek word for withdrawal), as "hermits" (from the Greek word for desert), and as "monks" (from the Greek word for solitary.) The "desert fathers" were an influential group of these monks who settled in the Egyptian desert.

The way of life in these early groups led to the formation of the first Christian monasteries. Under the direction of men like Saint Pachomius and Saint Anthony Abbot, practical matters of communal living were addressed. This allowed men and women to steep themselves in a world of contemplation and prayer with a group of like-minded friends—a tradition that has led thousands, over the centuries, to embrace a deepening peace and to move into transcendental states of joy and ecstasy.

As the number of monasteries grew and spread in Europe, several of them would become linked by following the same "rule" (a guide to how the community should live.) One of the most well known was the rule of Saint Benedict who founded a monastery in Italy in about 530. Benedict directed that a monk's life should be one of both prayer and work. Under the guidance of the popes of Rome, many monks became scholars and teachers as well. At a time when few laymen could read or write, it was the monks who preserved much classical learning which would otherwise have been lost.

Monks prayed for the souls of the dead along with their more practical duties of caring for the sick and feeding the poor. Christian monasteries in the Middle Ages provided almost all the medical skill available at the time.

Saint Francis, perhaps the most beloved of all the Christian saints, was devoted to living as closely as possible to the spirit of Christ. He founded an order that was based on absolute poverty, insisting upon humility and love as the basis for a deeper experience of Christ. A friend named Clare founded a similar order for women.

# Saint Pachomius (292 - 346)

A native of Egypt, Pachomius established the first Christian monastic community, outlining a schedule of shared meals, work, prayer, and discipline.

As a youth of twenty, Pachomius was inducted into the emperor's army and while stationed in Thebes he met great kindness from some Christians there. The experience became embedded in his mind and led to his conversion. After being baptized, he became the disciple of a desert hermit named Palemon. Together they led a life of extreme austerity and total dedication, combining manual labor with unceasing prayer that they practiced day and night.

After some time, Pachomius felt called to build a cell on the banks of the Nile. Palemon helped him build it and remained with him for a while. In a short time some one hundred monks came to join him and Pachomius began to organize them with principles that he saw necessary for communal living. So prevalent was the desire of those who met him to emulate the life of Pachomius and his monks, that he was obliged to establish ten other monasteries for men and two nunneries for women. Before his death there were seven thousand monks in his houses.

# Saint Anthony the Abbot

Two Greek philosophers ventured out into the Egyptian desert to the place where Anthony lived. When they got there, Anthony asked them why they had come to talk to such a foolish man. They were Greek and came from the world's most admired civilization, while he was a man who wore animal skins for clothes, who refused to bathe, and who lived on bread and water. They were philosophers, educated in languages and rhetoric, and he had not even attended school. In their eyes, he said to them, he must appear very foolish.

But the Greek philosophers had heard great stories of Anthony. They had heard that his words comforted all those who suffered and that his wisdom brought great joy. They assured him that they had come to him because he was a wise man.

Anthony guessed that what they wanted was to engage in arguments about Christianity and the value of asceticism, and he refused to play their game. He told them that if they truly thought him wise, they ought to imitate the life he led. "Had I gone to you, I should have imitated you, but, since you have come to me, become what I am—a Christian."

# Saint Benedict (480 - 547)

As a youth Benedict was sent to complete his education and study rhetoric in Rome, but he grew dismayed by the lack of discipline and the lackadaisical attitude of his fellow students. Afraid for his soul he gave up his inheritance, fled Rome, and moved to a small village.

When called to an even deeper solitude he went to the mountains to become a hermit under the direction of an ascetic named Romanus. He lived in a cave for three years and is reported to have been fed by a raven. After years of prayer, word of him brought nearby monks to ask for his leadership. He warned them he would be too strict for them, but they insisted. Later, when his warning proved true and they tried to poison him, Benedict blessed the cup of poison and rendered it harmless.

Towards the end of his life, Benedict wrote a rule for his order which he called Benedictines, and eventually he established twelve monasteries. He taught a simple life of prayer and work, and his early strict regimen was replaced with one that was far gentler. He called it "a school of the Lord's service, in which we wish to order nothing harsh or rigorous."

# Saint Francis of Assisi (1182 - 1226)

Francis was born in Assisi, a town in central Italy. His father was a wealthy cloth merchant, but Francis, a fun-loving young man, was infatuated by the lore of the troubadours. When he was about twenty he joined in a local war, was captured, imprisoned for a year, and subsequently suffered a long illness. Upon recovering, he bought a horse and armor and went off to fight again, this time in the service of a famous knight. Before reaching the battlefront he had a dream in which he was told to turn back and to "serve the master rather than the man." Francis turned around, went back to Assisi, and immediately began to lead a more austere life. Dressed in a simple robe he devoted his life to the sick and the unloved. He once traded places with a beggar. Another time he overcame a strong aversion and kissed a leper—who according to some was Jesus.

One day while praying in the chapel, Francis heard a voice that said to him, "Francis, go and repair my house." Not understanding the implications of this message Francis set about making physical repairs to the small tumbledown church of San Damoano, selling his horse and some of his father's cloth to buy materials. Confronted by his angry father, Francis took off all his clothes and standing naked

before his father, disowned him in deference to his spiritual father, saying "Our Father who art in heaven… I want to go to heaven naked."

After listening to a reading of the Gospel in which Jesus tells a rich man to sell all he has and give it to the poor, Francis refused to own anything at all. He begged for food and shelter on a daily basis, and his love for chivalry was changed to love of poverty, which he lovingly referred to as his Lady Poverty. He modeled his life on the example of Jesus and was always joyful, paying homage to every animate and inanimate creature of God.

After attracting a number of followers he wrote a rule based on the teachings of Christ, and a few years later he helped found a second order for women which became known as the Poor Clares. He then wrote a rule for a third order for lay men and women who were unable to live a communal life. The three orders spread quickly throughout the world.

Francis was so dedicated that he longed to experience all that Jesus had felt. One day a winged seraph appeared and granted his wish. Francis was burned with the stigmata, the five wounds of Jesus in his hands, feet and side. Two years later he died.

# Saint Clare of Assisi (1194 - 1253)

Clare was the daughter of a count and countess in Assisi. After hearing Saint Francis preach in the streets one day, she went up to him and expressed her desire to live, as he did, for God; and the two became close friends. On the following Palm Sunday the bishop of Assisi presented her with a palm which Clare took as a sign from God and together with her cousin Pacifica, she left her home that night. She cut off her hair, renounced all her possessions, and began her new life.

Clare meditated daily and lived in strict adherence to the rule of Saint Francis—a life that was extremely simple and void of worldly pleasures. She depended solely on alms, trusting in God to provide all that was needed. Clare founded the Order of Poor Clares which she led for forty years. Everywhere the Franciscans established themselves in Europe, there also went the Poor Clares.

Clare was a gentle woman with a great love of nature. She ran the nunnery with a sense of joyousness. When Saint Francis died he asked that his body be carried back to Assisi via her nunnery so that Clare could bathe his feet.

# Visionaries and Mystics

The word "mysticism" is derived from the Greek mystikos, which means "to enter the mysteries" and implies entering various states of ecstatic experience. These states are real states. They are the result, not of turning away from the world in a physical sense, but rather of turning inward.

Many writings have been discovered from the times in which Jesus lived that are deeply mystical in nature. From them we can assume that Jesus was teaching on many levels. As he traveled around from place to place he spoke to all those who would listen. In the eyes of some he was seen as a miracle-worker and an inspired speaker. However, he clearly worked more deeply with those who truly wanted to discover the nature of their being and to experience their own relationship with God. In reading the Gospel of Thomas it becomes clear to many that a significant part of Jesus' teaching was about the inner experiences and mysteries.

As the story of Christianity has unfolded, many men and women—those we know as Christian visionaries and mystics—have turned within to find God. Some have stumbled unknowingly upon mysterious doors that lead them inward, and some have journeyed there with intention. The inner journey is a complex and arduous one, but its rewards are truly those of the Kingdom of God. The poetry and ecstatic writing of the great visionaries and mystics is testament to the joyful states that are attainable.

Saint Teresa of Avila is one of those who seems to have moved purposefully into her inner world. It may have been the innocence and purity of her heart that led her there for she likens God to a dear friend and mystical lover. John of the Cross calls out from the depths of his soul, of its dark nights and sublime heights, while Catherine of Sienna describes in detail the mystical experiences of her heart. Hildegard of Bingen was a visionary who was commanded by God to write. Her poems and hymns are full of symbols and invented languages that speak allegorically of the mysteries of the inner worlds.

# Gospel of Thomas

During the last century numerous ancient Gospel writings were discovered. Most famous of these is the Gospel of Thomas. Sometimes called the "fifth gospel," it begins with the words, "These are the secret sayings which the living Jesus spoke and which Didymos Judas Thomas wrote down."

The Gospel takes the form of a collection of sayings that are beautiful in their simplicity and clearly mystical in origin. Unlike the Gospels of Matthew, Mark, Luke, and John, which describe many of the events of Christ's life, the Gospel of Thomas is simply a collection of the spiritual teachings of a master.

There is some debate about when this Gospel was composed. Some say that since it consists of mostly original material, it must have been transcribed from an oral tradition and therefore may have been written as early as the year 50.

In the Gospel of Thomas we meet Jesus the mystic who teaches that the "Kingdom of God" is right here, right now. He is a sage, a humble man with a powerful message who directs his listeners to turn inward. He encourages them to find the eternal treasure that lies hidden within each human soul.

# Saint Teresa of Avila (1515 - 1582)

Teresa's father was a rigidly honest and deeply pious man. Her mother loved romance novels and, because her husband objected to them, she hid the books. This put Teresa in the middle—especially since she liked the novels too. Her father told her never to lie but her mother told her not to tell her father. Later Teresa said she was always afraid that no matter what she did she was bound to do everything wrong.

When Teresa was sixteen, her father decided she was out of control and sent her to a convent school. At first she hated it but eventually she began to enjoy herself—partly because of her growing love for God, and partly because the convent was a lot less strict than her father was.

After struggling with her health for many years, she suffered an illness that was so severe a grave was dug for her, and after which she was paralyzed for three years. She never completely regained good health. What Teresa discovered, she would later say, is that "Prayer is an act of love, words are not needed. Even if sickness distracts from thoughts, all that is needed is the will to love."

# Saint John of the Cross (1542 - 1591)

After his father died, John's mother kept the family together as they wandered homeless in search of work. John often went hungry in the middle of the wealthiest city in Spain. At fourteen he took a job caring for hospital patients who suffered from incurable diseases and madness. It was through his experiences with poverty and suffering that he learned to search for beauty and happiness not in the world, but in God.

John joined the Carmelite order and befriended Teresa of Avila who asked him to help with a reform movement. The Carmelites were threatened by this and some members of his own order kidnapped him. He was locked in a cell six feet by ten and beaten three times a week by the monks. There was only one tiny window high up near the ceiling, yet in that unbearable dark, cold, and desolation, his love and faith were like fire and light. He had nothing left but God—and this deep love brought John his greatest joy in that tiny cell.

Having managed to escape he hid in a convent infirmary where he read his poetry to the nuns. From then on John's life was devoted to sharing and explaining his personal experience of God's love.

# Saint Catherine of Sienna (1347 - 1380)

The twenty-fifth child of a wool dyer in northern Italy, Catherine began to have mystical experiences when she was six, seeing guardian angels as clearly as the people they protected. She lived through the Black Death, famine, and numerous civil wars, and at a young age she began to sense the troubled society around her and wanted to help. Childishly she dreamed of dressing up like a man to become a friar, and more than once she ran into the street to kiss the ground where Dominicans had walked.

As a young woman she experienced what she described in her letters as a "mystical marriage" with Christ. She had a series of visions after which she heard a command to leave the convent and enter the public life of the world. Religious politics had pitted one pope against another, and Catherine, who was spontaneous, unafraid of authority, and fearless in the face of death, was very influential in persuading the pope in Avignon to return to Rome.

During her life Catherine had numerous visions and long ecstasies, but she is most remembered for her inspired writings.

# Saint Hildegard von Bingen (1098 - 1179)

As was customary with the tenth child in a family that could not count on enough food, Hildegard was dedicated at birth to the Church. At the age of three she began to have visions of luminous objects. She soon realized this ability was unique and hid the gift for many years.

When she turned eight her family sent the strange girl to an anchoress named Jutta for her education. Anchors were ascetics who shut themselves off from the world. They lived inside small rooms, usually adjacent to a church, so that they could follow the services, with only a small window acting as a link to the rest of humanity. Because they were essentially dead to the world, anchors received their last rights before their confinement. Hildegard entered Jutta's cell through a tiny door.

For many years the only people she told about her visions were Jutta and another monk. However, she eventually had a vision in which she was commanded to write down everything she observed. The writings seemed to come from God, and crowds of people flocked to hear the words of wisdom that came from her lips.

# Missionaries and Samaritans

With hearts that were overflowing with a message of love, many Christian saints moved into service. Through their acts of charity and compassion they expressed their gratitude and thanksgiving.

Missionaries and samaritan saints of Christianity are those who have carried the spirit of Christ to others. They have in some sense lit a torch that burns from generation to generation and throughout the world. Simple acts of kindness carry a simple message, and the message of love that Jesus preached was reinforced with every samaritan act.

The beautiful story of Saint Martin of Tours is an example of a samaritan at work. Wishing to help those in distress, he carried the Christian message around the countryside of Gaul. Seeing a beggar one day, he tore his cloak in two and gave half to the man to keep him warm. That night Martin had a dream in which he heard Jesus say to him, "What thou hast done for that poor man, thou hast done for me." Although the beggar may not have changed his faith, he very likely associated with Saint Martin a sense of being cared for.

In the years after the death of Jesus, Saint Paul and others transformed him from a possible Messiah of the Jews into the Savior of mankind. Christianity became a religion whose potential congregation encompassed the entire population of the known world. The spreading of the word was always an essential Christian passion.

The diaspora of the Jews in the year 70 also saw the dispersal of the earliest Christians from their center in Jerusalem, for they had always refused to ally themselves with the official religion of the Roman Empire. As Christians scattered around the Mediterranean they spread their message with a sense of urgency, making converts when and where they could. Their survival depended upon a strong movement. As the new message of love that the movement carried was quite revolutionary, it attracted many who objected in their hearts to the power Rome was wielding. In the fourth century Constantine declared Christianity the official religion of the empire and Christian proselytizing was sanctioned. With the gradual disintegration of Roman power and the ensuing barbarian invasions, missionaries began to push further north, west, and east from Rome to convert the scattered tribes who had so fiercely rejected Roman rule.

Saint Patrick, who is so famous for his work in Ireland, was actually sent there as a slave. Having escaped, he later returned as a bishop to one of the few countries in Europe that Rome had not conquered. The Church he introduced was embraced by the Irish and it was these Celtic Christians that helped keep Christianity alive when barbarians later swept through Britain.

As the Western world expanded its influence over many centuries it was people like Saint Francis Xavier who carried the Christian religion to far off lands, converting people everywhere with a heart that reached out to help those in need. It is said the Saint Francis Xavier had the gift of tongues, and although it is possible that he was able to speak in any language, it is more likely that the universality of his message transcended language and was spoken from heart to heart. It was, after all, a message of love.

# Saint Martin of Tours (316 - 397)

Martin joined the Roman imperial army when he was fifteen, served as the emperor's bodyguard, and became an officer. During this time he was baptized a Christian, and when he was eighteen, just before a battle began, Martin announced that his faith prohibited him from fighting. Charged with cowardice he was jailed by his superiors. As punishment they planned to stand him in the front line of the battle, but the invaders sued for peace, the battle never occurred, and Martin was released from military service.

Trying to live his faith, he refused to let his servant wait on him. Once, while on horseback in Gaul, he encountered a beggar and having nothing to give but the clothes on his back, he cut his heavy officer's cloak in half, and gave it to the beggar. Later he had a vision of Christ wearing the cloak.

Martin preached and evangelized throughout the countryside of Gaul where the locals were holding strongly to their old beliefs. They tried, in vain, to intimidate him by dressing up as Roman gods and appearing to him at night. Martin merely laughed at their efforts and continued to win converts. He destroyed old temples and built churches in their place.

# Saint Patrick (387 - 461)

Saint Patrick of Ireland is one of the world's most popular saints. Born in Scotland, he was captured when he was fourteen or so and taken to Ireland as a slave to herd and tend sheep. Ireland at this time was a land of Druids and pagans. During these early years, Patrick learned the language and practices of the people who held him.

His captivity lasted until he was twenty when he escaped after having a dream in which he was told to travel to the coast. At a small harbor he found some sailors who took him back to Britain where he reunited with his family and spent many years studying in the Church before returning to Ireland.

Patrick was a humble, pious, gentle man. With love and total trust in God, he preached throughout Ireland. He and his disciples converted thousands of people and began building churches all over the country. Kings, their families, and entire kingdoms converted to Christianity.

Patrick used the shamrock to explain the Trinity, and it has been associated with him and the Irish since that time.

# Saint Francis Xavier (1506 - 1552)

Having been convinced in his youth that he wanted to become a Jesuit, Saint Francis Xavier became a missionary and traveled to Goa, India, where he is said to have converted the entire city. He preached in the street, worked with the sick, and taught children their catechism.

Working against great difficulties that included language problems, inadequate funds, and lack of cooperation from European officials, he left the mark of his zeal and energy on areas which have remained Christian for centuries.

He was tremendously successful as a missionary in India, the East Indies, and Japan. He is said to have dined with headhunters, washed the sores of lepers, and baptized ten thousand in a single month. He tolerated the most appalling conditions on long sea voyages, enduring extremes of heat and cold, and wherever he went he would seek out and help the poor and forgotten. Saint Francis Xavier traveled thousands of miles, mostly on his bare feet, and he saw much of the Far East.

# Legends

Over the passage of time, tales of certain individuals were retold so often, and in such a fashion, that the men and women involved became legends. Tales of their deeds inspired hope and trust. Sometimes their stories became merged with older myths and legends. The stories of some saints play a particular role in our lives, having become the basis for holidays and festivals. As icons there are saints who protect us in troubled times or in the face of mystery.

Saint Valentine and Saint Nicholas are two very popular examples of saints whose commemoration falls on ancient festivals. The Church found it necessary to keep the festival but change the reason for it.

In the early days of the development of Christianity, it was sometimes the case that ancient cult figures simply could not be dislodged from the popular mind. It so happened that stories—like that of Saint George defeating the dragon and Saint Christopher carrying children across a river—actually evolved from ancient tales to create new legendary figures. The new stories eventually became imbedded in the mind and popular saints replaced more ancient heros.

# Saint George

Several stories have been attached to Saint George, the most well known of which tells of a dragon that lived in a lake in Libya. Whole armies of men had pitted themselves against this fierce creature and had gone down in painful defeat. The monster ate two sheep each day, and when these became scarce, lots were drawn in local villages and maidens were substituted for sheep. Into this ill-fated country came Saint George.

Hearing the story on a day when a princess was about to be fed to the dragon, he crossed himself and rode to battle against the serpent, which he killed with a single blow of his lance. George then held forth with a magnificent sermon, converted the local villagers, and was given a large reward by the king. This he distributed to the poor before riding away.

Due to his chivalrous behavior, devotion to Saint George became extremely popular in the Europe. In the fifteenth century his feast day was as popular and important as Christmas.

# Saint Christopher

Christopher was a giant and so proud of his size and strength that he would take service with no one but the most powerful monarch in the world. Having set out to find this man, he served his king until he saw him making the sign of the cross at the mention of the devil. He then served Satan, thinking him to be more powerful. When he saw Satan tremble at the sight of a cross, he went searching again and finally found a hermit who told him about the Christian faith. Christopher refused to be bound by prayers and fasting but was told that if he could not worship, he could serve. The hermit took him to a river and told him to carry on his shoulders all those who wished to cross.

Christopher pulled up a tree for a staff and day and night carried over all those who wanted to cross to the other side. One night a child approached him. Christopher lifted him on his shoulders and entered the river. The waters rose and the wind roared and the child grew heavier and heavier. When at last they reached the bank the child said he had carried over him who made the world. Christopher fell down in prayer and began to praise the Christians saying his name was Christopher for he had carried Christ. Later, after many sufferings and terrible tortures he was imprisoned and beheaded.

# Saint Valentine (d. 270)

In the early days of Christianity, the Roman Emperor Claudius made it a crime, punishable by death, to associate with Christians. At this time, there was a man named Valentinus who was dedicated to Christ, and not even the threat of death could keep him from practicing his beliefs. It is sometimes said that he secretly married young couples who were in love but did not have parental permission. In 270, Valentinus was taken prisoner and condemned to die.

During the last weeks of his life a jailer knocked at his cell door clutching his blind daughter, Julia, in his arms. He appealed to Valentinus to treat her blindness. Valentinus gave the man his word he would do his best. He spent much time with her and taught her about Jesus, although he could not cure her blindness.

On the eve of his death, Valentinus wrote a farewell note to Julia, urging her to stay close to God. His sentence was carried out the next day, February 14, near a gate that was later named Porta Valentini in his memory. When Julia opened the note, which was signed "From Your Valentine," her blindness was miraculously healed. In later days February 14 was named Saint Valentine's Day, a day on which messages of affection are exchanged.

# Saint Nicholas of Myra (270 - 345)

Serving as a bishop in Asia Minor, Nicholas was generous to the poor and was a special protector of the innocent and wronged. Many stories grew up around him prior to his becoming Santa Claus.

Upon hearing that a man had fallen on such hard times that he was planning to sell his daughters into prostitution, Nicholas went by night to the house and threw three bags of gold in through the window, saving the girls.

Another tale tells that he raised to life three young boys who had been murdered and pickled in a barrel of brine to hide the crime. This led to his patronage of children.

Yet another tale tells that he induced some thieves to return their plunder helping them to repent and change their ways.

During a voyage to the Holy Lands, it is said that a fierce storm blew up, threatening the ship he was on. He prayed and the storm calmed—hence his patronage of sailors and those who work on the sea.

# Saint Joan of Arc (1412 - 1431)

Joan of Arc was born to pious parents of the French peasant class. At a very early age, she began to hear the voices of various saints, namely Saint Michael, Saint Catherine, and Saint Margaret.

At first the messages were personal and general, but then came an order. She was told to go to the King of France and help him to regain his kingdom. The English king at that time was after the throne of France and was helping the French king's nobles to overthrow him.

After overcoming opposition from churchmen and courtiers, the seventeen-year-old girl was given a small army with which she enjoyed a series of spectacular military successes. Finally the King was crowned, with Joan standing at his side. Soon afterwards she was captured and sold to the English. The French did nothing to save her, and after months of imprisonment a tribunal tried her. She refused to retract her assertion that it was the saints of God who commanded her to do what she had done, and she was condemned to death as a heretic, sorceress, and adulteress, and burned at the stake.

# Afterword

A story has been passed down that was told by the Desert Fathers. It concerns two old men who had dwelt together for many years and who never quarreled. One day one of them said to the other, "Let us pick a quarrel with one another like so many men do."

"I do not know how quarrels arise," said his companion.

"Well," said the first man, "I will put a brick down here between us and I will say, 'This is mine.' Then you can say, 'No it is not; it is mine.' Then we will be able to have a quarrel."

So they placed the brick between them and the first man said, "This is mine."

His companion answered, "This is not so, for it is mine."

To this, the first man answered, "If it is so and the brick is yours, then take it and go your way."
And so they were not able to have a quarrel.

Much has been written about the Christian saints. One of the aspects that stands out most profoundly about them all is their wholehearted devotion to a simple message about the one they love above all others.

Twenty centuies ago Jesus spoke in simple words to ordinary men and women. He gave them a promise and awakened in their hearts a desire to come close to him. Throughout his life he taught through his actions, and as he met his death he rose to Heaven.

"Come, follow me," he had said to his disciples, and although the way was not easy to see, they followed. Jesus and the many, many men and women who later followed him, have created a path that is now recognized as one of the world's great religions.

It is a path based upon the simple principles of love and sharing. It is a path whose rewards are eternal and fulfilling. The lives of the saints are a testament to the joy of following Christ. The fondness with which we remember them keeps his love alive.

# Acknowledgements

Cover: *Mocking of Christ* (detail) by Fra Angelico; Convent of San Marco, Florence.

Page 4: *Saint Michael* by Carlo Crivelli; National Gallery, London.

Page 6: *Paradise* by Giovanni di Paolo; Metropolitan Museum of Art, New York.

Page 9: *The Crucifixion* by Dionissi; Tretyakov Gallery, Moscow.

Page 10: *Entry into Jerusalem* by Fra Angelico; Convent of San Marco, Florence.

Page 15: *Three Saints* by Bartolomeo Montagna; National Gallery, London.

Page 16: *Angel with a Lute* by Melozzo da Forli; Vatican Museum, Rome.

Page 18: *Saint Michael* by Luca Giordano; Gemaldegalerie, Berlin.

Page 21: *Annunciation* by Fra Angelico; Museo Diocesano, Cortona, Italy.

Page 22: *The Mystic Nativity* by Botticelli; National Gallery, London.

Page 25: *Christ Preaching and Bystanders* by Pietro Perugino; Cappella Sistina, Vatican.

Page 26: *The Virgin Annunciate* by Naddo Ceccarelli; Noortman Ltd., London.

Page 29: *Meeting of Joachim and Anna* by Giovanni da Milano; Rinuccini Chapel, Santa Croce, Florence.

Page 30: *The Baptism of Christ* by Alessandro Allori; Accademia Gallery, Florence.

Page 33: *Noli Me Tangere* by Fra Angelico; Convent of San Marco, Florence.

Page 34: *Jesus Surrounded by Disciples at the Sermon on the Mount* by Fra Angelico; San Marco, Florence.

Page 37: *The Pentecost* by Giotto; The Scrovegni Chapel, Padua.

Page 38: *The Miraculous Draft of Fishes* by Antoniazzo Romano; Musee du Petit Palais, Avignon.

Page 41: *The Calling of the Apostles Peter and Andrew* by Duccio di Buoninsegna; National Gallery of Art, Washington D.C.

Page 42: *Saint James* by Andrea Del Sarto; Uffizi Gallery, Florence.

Page 45: *Rendering of the Tribute Money* (detail) by Masaccio; Brancacci Chapel, Santa Maria del Carmine, Florence.

Page 46: *The Incredulity of Saint Thomas* by Guercino; Vatican Museum, Rome.

Page 49: *Saint James the Less* by El Greco; Art Institute of Chicago, Chicago.

Page 50: *Saint John the Evangelist on Patmos* by Hans Burgkmair the Elder; Alte Pinakothek, Munich.

Page 52: *The Evangelist Matthew* from an illuminated Gospel book; British Library, London.

Page 55: *Saint Mark Cutting a Pen* by Boucicaut Master; Pierpont Morgan Library, New York.

Page 56: *Saint Luke from the MacDurnan Gospels*; Lambeth Palace Library, London.

Page 59: *St. John the Evangelist* from a fresco at Abbey Church of Sant'Antonio di Ranverso, Italy.

Page 60: *Crucifixion of Saint Peter* by Michelangelo; Vatican Museums, Rome.

Page 62: *The Stoning of Saint Stephen* by Fra Angelico; Pulci and Berardi Chapel, Santa Croce.

Page 65: *Saint Denis* by Boucicaut Master; Musee Jacquemart-Andre, Paris.

Page 66: *Saint Thomas Becket*; Biblioteca Estense e Universitaria, Modena.

Page 68: *The Martyrdom of Ursula and her Maidens* by Memling; Keystone Press Agency, Montreal.

Page 70: *The Apoltheosis of Saint Ursula* by Virrore Carpaccio; Accademia, Venice.

Page 73: *Saint Catherine of Alexandria*; Pinacoteca Di Brera, Milan.

Page 74: *Gregory the Great*; Pushkin Museum, St. Petersburg.

Page 78: *Saint Peter Preaching* by Fra Angelico; Museo di San Marco, Florence.

Page 81: *Saint Paul's Conversion*; Lower Saxony Museum, Hannover.

Page 82: *Saint Jerome* by Domenico Ghirlandaio; Ognissanti, Florence.

Page 85: *Saint Augustine* by Sandro Botticelli; Chiesa di Ognissanti, Florence.

Page 86: *Vision of Saint Thomas Aquinas* by Sassetta; Vatican Museums, Rome.

Page 88: *Saint John the Baptist in the Wilderness* by Geertgen tot Sint Jans; Staatliche Museum, Berlin.

Page 91: *The Meeting of Saint Anthony and Saint Paul* by Sassetta; National Gallery of Art, Washington D.C.

Page 92: *Saint Francis Embracing Poverty* by Giotto; Scala Istituto Fotografico Editoriale, Florence.

Page 94: *Coptic Abbot Menas with Christ*; Louvre, Paris.

Page 97: *Saint Anthony Abbot* by Francisco de Zurbaran; Meridiana Pavilion, Florence.

Page 98: *Saint Benedict in Prayer* by Master of Messkirch; Staatsgalerie, Stuttgart.

Page 101: *Saint Francis of Assisi Preaching to the Birds* by Giotto; Louvre, Paris.

Page 104: *The Stigmata of Saint Francis* by Master of St. Francis Bardi; Uffizi Gallery, Florence.

Page 105: *Saint Clare of Assisi*; ET Archive.

Page 106: From the Psalter of St Louis and Blanche of Castile; Edimedia, Paris.

Page 109: *Hildegard von Bingen's Fourth Vision* © Alexander Roob; Berlin.

Page 110: *The Apostle Thomas* by Nicolas Frances; Eitan Simanor, Jerusalem.

Page 113: *The Death of Saint Clare* by Master of Heiligenkreuz; National Gallery of Art, Washington D.C.

Page 114: *The Anticipation of the Coming of Christ by Saint John of the Cross* by Nicolo Lorenese; Sta. Maria della Vittoria, Rome.

Page 117: *Saint Catherine of Siena Dictating Her Dialogues to Raymond of Capua* by Giovanni di Paolo; Detroit Institute of Arts, Detroit.

Page 118: *Inflamed by a Fiery Light*; Courtesy of Angelika Engelhardt-Rotthaus, Bingen.

Page 120: *Saint Basil Dictating His Doctrine* by Francisco de Herrera the Elder; Louvre, Paris.

Page 123: *The Baptism of Clovis* by Master of Saint Giles; National Gallery of Art, Washington D.C.

Page 126: *Saint Martin and the Beggar* by El Greco; National Gallery of Art, Washington D.C.

Page 124: *Saint Francois Xavier*; Mary Evans Picture Library, London.

Page 129: *Saint Patrick Baptising Christian Converts*, Lonbard School; San Patrizio, Colzate, Italy.

Page 130: *Saint Francis Xavier* by Bartolome Esteban Murrillo; Wadsworth Athenaeum, Harford.

Page 132: *Saint Nicolas Saves a Storm-Tossed Ship* by Gentile da Fabriano; Pinacoteca Vaticana, Rome.

Page 134: *Saint George and the Dragon* by Raphael; National Gallery of Art, Washington D.C.

Page 137: *Saint Christopher* by Master of the Embroidered Foliage; Gemaldegalerie, Dresden.

Page 138: *Saint Valentine*; Mary Evans Picture Library, London.

Page 141: *Saint Nicholas*; Biblioteca Nazionale, Naples.

Page 142: *Joan of Arc and the Sword of Deliverance* by Dante Gabriel Rossetti.

Page 144: *Christ Appearing to Saint Peter on the Appian Way* by Annibale Carracci; National Gallery, London.

# Index of Saints